Investigate Science

Down to Earth

by Melissa Stewart

Content Adviser: Jan Jenner, Ph.D.

Reading Adviser: Rosemary G. Palmer, Ph.D.,
Department of Literacy, College of Education,
Boise State University

COMPASS POINT BOOKS ✦ MINNEAPOLIS · MINNESOTA

Visit Compass Point Books on the Internet at *www.compasspointbooks.com* or e-mail your request to
custserv@compasspointbooks.com

Photographs ©: Ariel Skelley/Corbis, cover (middle); Peter Hulme/Ecoscene/Corbis, cover (background);
PhotoDisc, cover (bottom), 1, 12; Gregg Andersen, 4, 5, 6, 7 (top), 8, 9, 10, 11 (all), 13, 14, 20, 21, 23; E.R.
Degginger/Bruce Coleman Inc., 7 (bottom); James P. Rowan, 16, 24; Jeff Foott/Tom Stack & Associates, 17;
Ann & Rob Simpson, 18; Kent & Donna Dannen, 19; Robert W. Ginn/Unicorn Stock Photos, 22; Creatas, 25.

Editor: Christianne C. Jones
Photo Researcher: Svetlana Zhurkina
Designer: The Design Lab
Illustrator: Jeffrey Scherer

Library of Congress Cataloging-in-Publication Data
Stewart, Melissa.
Down to earth / by Melissa Stewart.
   p. cm. — (Investigate science)
Summary: Introduces the components of soil, patterns of change, and erosion.
ISBN 0-7565-0595-X (Hardcover)
1. Soils—Juvenile literature. 2. Soil ecology—Juvenile literature.
[1. Soils. 2. Soil ecology. 3. Ecology.] I. Title. II. Series.
S591.3.S728 2004
631.4—dc22   2003018844

Note to Readers: To learn about rocks and soil, scientists observe them closely. They draw and write about everything they see. Later, they use their drawings and notes to help them remember exactly what they observed.

This book will help you study rocks and soil like a scientist. To get started, you will need to get a notebook and a pencil.

Before you start collecting rocks or digging up soil, make sure you get permission from an adult. Also get permission from the person who owns the land.

In the Doing More section in the back of the book, you will find step-by-step instructions for more fun science experiments and activities.

In this book, words that are defined in the glossary are in **bold** the first time they appear in the text.

Table of Contents

As you read this book, be on the lookout for these special symbols:

Read directions *very carefully.*

Ask an adult for help.

Turn to the Doing More section in the back of the book.

Look Down at the Ground

Go outside and look down at the ground. Unless you're standing on pavement, **soil** is everywhere. Soil contains all sorts of surprises. You can find them if you look closely.

Use a piece of string or rope about 5 feet (1.5 meters) long to rope off an area that has grass and plants. Sit down and **observe** the ground as a scientist would. How many different kinds of plants grow in the area? Do you see any insects or other animals? What are these creatures doing? Observe the area for 30 minutes, and draw everything you see.

Return to the spot at different times of the day and on days with different kinds of weather. Do you notice any differences in the number or kinds of creatures in your area?

Drawing and writing down what you observe helps you work like a scientist. Your notes will help you remember what you studied so you can learn more.

Don't be afraid
to get a little dirty
while digging up
a soil sample!

Grab a shovel and dig up some soil from your roped-off area. Spread it out on an old white T-shirt. Look at the soil closely with a **hand lens.** Do you see any living things? How are they similar to the creatures you saw on the surface of the soil?

 How are they different?

Go to another area, and dig up some new soil. Put the new soil on another section of the T-shirt. Compare the creatures you see in the two samples. Draw pictures of the creatures, and ask an adult to help you identify them.

Earthworms are one creature you may find living in the soil.

A Closer Look at Soil

You see soil every day, but have you ever wondered what it's made of? To find out, put fresh soil in a large glass jar until it is about half full. Then add cold water until the jar is almost full. Screw on the lid and shake the jar for 30 seconds. Wait 20 minutes, and then draw what you see. Like a scientist's drawings, your picture will help you remember what you observed.

You should see layers of pebbles and rocky bits in your jar. Small, broken-up **rocks** are the main ingredient of soil. Look at the rocks closely. How are they arranged? Like a scientist, you are looking at the soil more closely to learn more about it.

Add water to the jar slowly so the soil doesn't spray out.

8

Scientists always pay careful attention to details, so take another look at the jar. You should see something floating on top of the water. It is tiny bits of rotting material. When plants, animals, and other living things die, they **rot** and become part of the soil.

Take the lid off the jar. Use a spoon to scoop out the rotting material, and place it on a plain white paper towel. Let the material dry. Then look at it with a hand lens. Can you identify any of the broken-down bits? Write or draw everything you see.

Look closely at the rocky bits in your soil samples. The largest ones are called **sand.** The medium-sized bits are called **silt.** Silt is just large enough to see with your eyes. The smallest bits are called **clay.** You need a hand lens to see them.

 Grab a handful of each soil sample, squeeze it, and watch what happens. Add a little water to each sample and squeeze them again. The table below will tell you what kind of soil you have.

	Mostly Sand	Mostly Silt	Mostly Clay
DRY	Feels gritty; falls apart	Feels smooth and silky; holds together	Feels slippery or sticky; breaks into hard clumps
WET	Holds together but crumbles easily	Holds together but cannot be rolled	Holds together and can be rolled

This small stream is slowly wearing down and breaking apart these rocks.

All of the rocky bits that make up soil started out as much larger rocks. Over many years, the rocks were slowly broken down. Even though rocks are hard and tough, crashing waves can slowly wear away rocky cliffs. Plant roots can push against a rock until it splits. Wind and ice can also break down rocks.

Look for places near your home where rocks are breaking apart. When scientists find spots like this, they draw pictures to show what is happening. You can also draw pictures to record what you see.

The flowing water has changed the shape of this rock.

What Is a Rock?

Rocks are all around us. Rocks are non-living objects made of natural materials. They are an important part of the natural world even though they aren't alive.

Make a list of ways that rocks are different from animals. Write down some ways they are different from plants. Compare your two lists. Use your lists to decide how you can tell whether something is alive.

Even though rocks aren't alive, they can still be very interesting. If you look closely at a rock, you might be surprised by what you see.

Find a small rock in your backyard or at a local park. Pick it up and observe it carefully. What color is it? Is it smooth or rough? Is it flat or round? Is it heavy or light? Does the rock have a smell? What happens when you drop it on the ground? Observe the rock. Do you see any patterns on the rock? Use a ruler to measure your rock. Then draw a picture of the rock.

It's easy to find rocks, especially small ones. Look under a tree or near a stream.

Observe your rock carefully to see how it is different from other rocks.

21

Rock piles are a great place to find different types of rocks. Always be careful when climbing on rocks.

For the next few days, collect small rocks wherever you go. Look for them in your backyard, on the school playground, at a local park, or in the woods. Try to find as many different kinds of rocks as you can.

How many different ways can you sort your rocks? Try arranging them by color, size, and shape. Then sort them from smoothest to roughest and from heaviest to lightest.

Sorting rocks can be like playing a game. Try sorting your rocks in at least three different ways.

As you collect rocks, look around and try to figure out how the rocks got there. Did they break off a much larger rock nearby? Did a river or stream carry them to the spot? Did someone dump the rocks there?

Now that you've examined rocks and soil, you have a better understanding of how soil and rocks form. Don't be afraid to dig in and get down to earth to learn more.

Did You Know?

Most rocks in a river or stream are smooth and round. The water wears down their jagged edges.

Doing More

Activity One

Page 7 showed you how to search for living things in the soil. Can you think of a common soil creature that has no eyes, breathes through its skin, and eats soil? The answer is an earthworm. To see how earthworms keep soil healthy, try this experiment.

1. Add a layer of soil and a layer of sand to a large plastic or glass jar. Spray water on each layer.

2. Place a few earthworms in the jar and cover them with dead leaves.

3. Draw a picture of the jar. Put the jar in a cool, dark place.

4. After a few hours, look at the jar. Draw a picture showing any changes you observe.

5. Check the jar again the next day. Draw another picture of what you see.

6. Add leaves, grass clippings, and fresh fruit to the jar. Which food do the earthworms eat first?

7. When the earthworms finish eating, bury them outside. They will be happier in their natural home.

leaves, grass, and worms

sand

soil

Activity Two

On page 15 you learned that scientists give three different names to the rocky bits in soil. To find out how the size of the rocky material in soil can affect how water flows through it, try this experiment.

1. Use masking tape and a marking pen to label three plates with the words Sandy Soil, Silty Soil, and Clay Soil.

2. Place a paper towel on each plate. Add 2 tablespoons of sandy soil to the first plate, 2 tablespoons of silty soil to the second plate, and 2 tablespoons of clay soil to the third plate.

3. Sprinkle 1 tablespoon of water over the first soil sample. Use a watch or timer with a second hand to measure how quickly the water drains through that soil sample.

4. Repeat step 3 for the other two soil samples. Then compare the three times. Do you think most plants grow better in sandy soil, silty soil, or clay soil? Why?

Activity Three

On page 23 you sorted rocks in many different ways. To practice your sorting skills, ask some friends to play a fun game.

1. Have your friends sit in a circle.

2. Give each person 10 rocks.

3. Place four more rocks in the middle.

4. At each turn, players try to think of a way one of their rocks matches a rock in the middle.

5. The player who matches all of his or her rocks first wins the game.

Glossary

clay soil with rocky bits so small you need a hand lens to see them

hand lens a tool that makes objects look bigger than they really are; sometimes called a magnifying glass

observe to use all five senses to gather information about the world

rock a nonliving object made of natural materials

rot to break down

sand soil with the largest rocky bits

silt soil with medium-sized rocky bits

soil a mixture of broken-up rocks and rotting plant and animal material

To Find Out More

At the Library

Bial, Raymond. *A Handful of Dirt*. New York: Walker, 2000.

Christian, Peggy. *If You Find a Rock*. New York: Harcourt Brace, 2000.

Flanagan, Alice K. *Rocks*. Minneapolis: Compass Point Books, 2001.

Flanagan, Alice K. *Soil*. Minneapolis: Compass Point Books, 2001.

Pellant, Chris. *The Best Book of Fossils, Rocks, and Minerals*. New York: Kingfisher, 2000.

On the Road

American Museum of Natural History

Central Park West at 79th St.

New York, NY 10024

The museum's Hall of Planet Earth features one of the world's best displays of rocks, minerals, and gemstones.

On the Web

For more information on **soil,** use FactHound to track down Web sites related to this book.

1. Go to *www.compasspointbooks.com/facthound*

2. Type in this book ID: **075650595X**

3. Click on the *Fetch It* button.

Your trusty FactHound will fetch the best Web sites for you!

Index

About the Author

Melissa Stewart earned a bachelor's degree in biology from Union College and a master's degree in science and environmental journalism from New York University. After editing children's science books for nearly a decade, she decided to become a full-time writer. She has written more than 50 science books for children and contributed articles to ChemMatters, Instructor, MATH, National Geographic World, Natural New England, Odyssey, Science World, and Wild Outdoor World. She also teaches writing workshops and develops hands-on science programs for schools near her home in Northborough, Massachusetts.